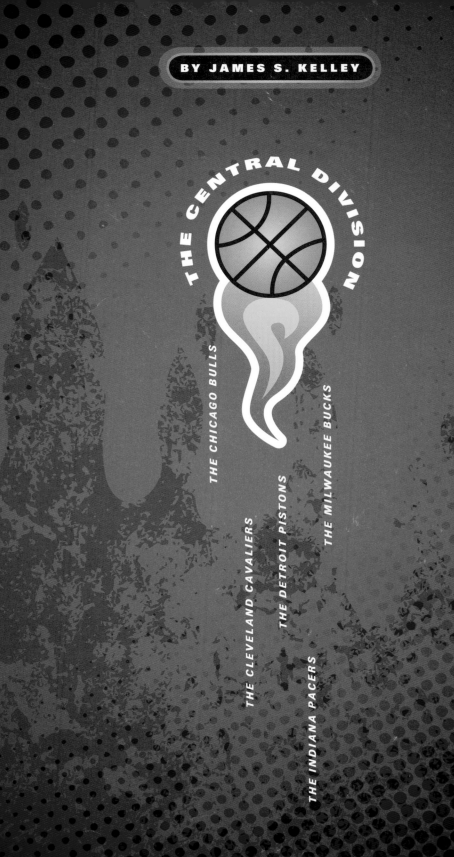

BY JAMES S. KELLEY

THE CENTRAL DIVISION

THE CHICAGO BULLS

THE CLEVELAND CAVALIERS

THE DETROIT PISTONS

THE INDIANA PACERS

THE MILWAUKEE BUCKS

Published in the United States of America by
The Child's World® • 1980 Lookout Drive
Mankato, MN 56003-1705
800-599-READ • www.childsworld.com

ACKNOWLEDGEMENTS

The Child's World®: Mary Berendes,
Publishing Director

The Design Lab: Kathleen Petelinsek,
Design and Page Production

Manuscript consulting and photo research by
Shoreline Publishing Group LLC.

PHOTOS

Cover: Corbis
Interior photos: AP/Wide World: 7, 13, 22;
Corbis: 18, 28, 30; Reuters: 4, 8, 10, 14, 17,
21, 25, 26, 32

**LIBRARY OF CONGRESS
CATALOGING-IN-PUBLICATION DATA**

Kelley, James S., 1960–

The Central division / by James S. Kelley.

p. cm.

Includes bibliographical references and index.

ISBN 978-1-59296-982-1
(library bound: alk. paper)

1. National Basketball Association—History—Juvenile literature. 2. Basketball—Middle
West—History—Juvenile literature. I. Title.

GV885.515.N37K444 2008

796.323'640973—dc22   2007034762

CONTENTS

*On the cover: LeBron "King" James
leaped from high school to the NBA
in 2003 and carried the Cleveland
Cavaliers to the NBA Finals in 2007.*

INTRODUCTION

The Central Division is so named for the geographic location of its five teams: the Chicago Bulls, Cleveland Cavaliers, Detroit Pistons, Indiana Pacers, and Milwaukee Bucks. But the Central is central in more ways than one. That's because, more often than not, the Central Division teams have been in the thick of the chase for the NBA championship.

In 2006–07, it was the Cleveland Cavaliers who advanced to the NBA Finals before falling to the San Antonio Spurs. To get to the Finals, the Cavaliers had to beat the division-rival Pistons, who have been title contenders for most of the 2000s.

Over the years, the current NBA Central teams have accounted for 10 NBA championships. And exciting young players such as LeBron James, Ben Gordon, and Michael Redd figure to keep the Central teams in the middle of the action for years to come.

CHAPTER ONE

THE CHICAGO BULLS

The Bulls were the dominant NBA team of the 1990s, winning six league championships.

Think "dynasty" in the NBA, and three **franchises** immediately come to mind: the Celtics of the 1960s and 1970s, the Lakers of the 1980s and early 2000s...and the Chicago Bulls of the 1990s. (The San Antonio Spurs of the

Michael Jordan was named the most valuable player of the league, the All-Star Game, and the NBA Finals during the Bulls' record season in 1995–96.

2000s are close, too, although they have yet to win back-to-back titles.) Think "superstar," and Michael Jordan's name is at the top—or very near the top—of the list. It was Jordan who was the heart and soul of the Bulls' six NBA championships in the nineties.

"Air Jordan" joined the Bulls as an athletic guard out of the University of North Carolina in 1984. He made an immediate impact as the league's rookie of the year that season, and he emerged as one of the NBA's top scorers. But Jordan's high-flying dunks weren't enough to make the Bulls a league champion. The team had to add other good players around him.

So the Bulls added important **role players** such as Scottie Pippen and Horace Grant. Then they hired former NBA player Phil Jackson as coach in 1989. Together, they helped Chicago capture the Central Division crown in 1990–91. The Bulls capped that season by defeating the Lakers in five games to win Chicago's first NBA title.

The Bulls added championships each of the next two years, too, before Jordan decided to try playing pro baseball. He was back in 1994–95, though, and by 1995–96, the Bulls had built the most powerful team in basketball history. With Jordan winning his record eighth scoring title (he went on to win 10 scoring titles, and his career average of 30.12 points per game is the highest in NBA history), the Bulls won 72 of their 82 regular-season games. They cruised to the first of three more league crowns in a row.

The last title was a six-game victory in the 1998 Finals against Utah. In Jordan's final game for the Bulls, he sank the championship-winning **jumper** with 5.2 seconds left.

Chicago's basketball history doesn't start and end with the Jordan years, though. The Bulls began play in 1966. The new squad quickly won over the city by posting the best record ever for an **expansion team**, 33–48. It was even good enough to make the **playoffs**, where the Bulls were eliminated by the St. Louis Hawks.

The Bulls did not build on that early success until the 1970s, however. That's when a new group of players led by Bob Love and Norm Van Lier led the team to four straight 50-win seasons and a regular spot in the NBA playoffs. Defensive specialist Jerry Sloan, one of the original expansion Bulls, was also a standout in this period. His hard-nosed play helped Chicago capture a division title in 1975.

Injuries and the retirement of key players ended the Bulls' competitive run, however. The team slid into a period of mediocrity until Jordan's arrival in 1984. After Jordan retired following the 1998

Luc Longley, who played center on three of Chicago's championship teams in the 1990s, was the first Australian to play in the NBA.

championship (he came back to play two
seasons for the Washington Wizards in
the early 2000s), Chicago slumped again.

Hall-of-Fame center Robert Parish finished a career that began in 1976–77 by playing one season for the Bulls in 1996–97. His 21 seasons are the most by a player in NBA history.

Jackson left at the same time as Jordan, and the team went through a series of coaches while missing the play-offs six consecutive seasons. In recent years, however, the Bulls have rekindled their winning ways. In 2004–05, they broke through under former NBA guard Scott Skiles to win 47 regular-season games—Chicago's most since Jordan's last year—and reach the **postseason**.

Chicago went out in the first round that season and the next. But in 2006–07, the Bulls won 49 games during the regular season, then won a playoff series for the first time since their 1998 title. It was a four-game sweep of the Miami Heat, who were the defending NBA champions.

In the next round, the division-rival Pistons ended Chicago's hopes for a dream season. Still, the current Bulls feature new stars such as young guards Ben Gordon (who averaged a team-leading 20.4 points per game in 2006–07) and Kirk Hinrich, and forward Luol Deng. They hope to return Chicago to success not seen since Michael Jordan's era.

Luol Deng is one of the young stars who has helped Chicago taste playoff success again.

CHAPTER TWO

THE CLEVELAND CAVALIERS

LeBron James and the Cavaliers rose above their Eastern Conference foes in 2007.

Michael Jordan was a star of the highest **magnitude** during his **heyday** with the Bulls in the 1990s. The player who most comes closest to Jordan these days in the NBA is Cleveland Cavaliers' forward LeBron James.

Like Jordan, James is a superb individual talent. But even more than that, his presence also makes everyone around him better. That was particularly true during the 2006–07 season, when James helped carry the Cavaliers all the way to the NBA Finals.

Cleveland won 50 games during the regular season that year and finished in second place in the Central Division. James was on the court for more minutes than any other player in the NBA, and his scoring average of 27.3 points per game ranked fourth in the league. In the playoffs, the Cavaliers had little trouble with the Wizards and Nets before facing a showdown with the Detroit Pistons for the right to play in the NBA Finals.

Cleveland dropped two close games to open the series before James took over. He played all but two minutes in Game 3, scoring 32 points to give the Cavaliers a crucial victory. Cleveland went on to win the next three games, too, and take the series.

Although the Cavaliers' championship hopes were dashed by the mighty Spurs in the Finals, they clearly had joined the ranks of the elite teams in the NBA in 2006–07. It was the most successful season in the history of a club that began in 1970.

The franchise did not have a promising beginning. The team went 15–67

Guard Mark Price was just about automatic from the free-throw line. In 12 seasons beginning in 1986–87 (nine of them were with the Cavaliers), he made an NBA-record 90.4 percent of 2,362 free-throw tries.

its first year and played in a half-empty arena. About the only thing the team had going for it was coach Bill Fitch's sense of humor. "I phoned Dial-a-Prayer," Fitch said during one bad losing streak, "but when they found out who it was, they hung up."

It took a long time, but Cleveland's prayers were finally answered. Led by center Nate Thurmond, the team enjoyed its first winning season in 1975–76. The Cavaliers captured the Central Division title and made it all the way to the Eastern Conference Finals. That remains the only division title in the club's history. Still, the Cavaliers suffered the first of many heartbreaks in the playoffs, falling to the Boston Celtics in six games.

From 1978 to 1987, Cleveland fielded consistently poor teams, never winning more games than it lost. Things began to improve in the late 1980s. The team chose talented young players such as Brad Daugherty, Ron Harper, and Mark Price in the **draft**. No matter how good the team got, however, it could not seem to get past the Chicago Bulls, led by Michael Jordan. In 1989, Jordan's jumper at the buzzer sent an excellent Cavaliers' squad home early from the playoffs. A few years later, in 1993, he did it again. The Cavaliers also fell to the Bulls in the 1992 Eastern Conference Finals.

Cleveland and Chicago staged some epic playoff battles in the early 1990s—although the Bulls had the upper hand.

In 2003–04, LeBron James became just the third rookie ever to average more than 20 points, 5 rebounds, and 5 assists per game. The other two: Oscar Robertson and Michael Jordan.

After these shattering defeats, the Cavaliers began the long process of **rebuilding**. Among their important signings was Lithuanian-born Zydrunas Ilgauskas. The 7-foot-3 center joined the team in 1997. In the 2002–03 season, he was an All-Star for the first time.

A cavalier is a soldier mounted on a horse. The franchise nickname was chosen by the fans in a newspaper contest.

The biggest news in Cleveland in a decade, though, came when the team drafted LeBron James in 2003.

James was only 18 at the time, but he quickly became one of the NBA's best, and most popular, players. Cleveland won only 17 games the season before James arrived, but improved to 35 wins his first year, then 42 in his second.

After the 2004–05 season, the team hired Mike Brown as coach. Cleveland also signed versatile guard Larry Hughes and veteran forward Donyell Marshall to help give "King James" a talented supporting cast. The Cavaliers were back in the playoffs in 2005–06. Then came the big year of 2006–07.

James earned his third consecutive All-Star selection that season to go along with several other awards he had already won. He was the NBA's rookie of the year in 2003–04, and was a first-team all-league choice in 2005–06.

With the team's success in 2006–07, though, LeBron became a megastar that even non-basketball fans knew. After that season, he could be seen on television hosting ESPN's Espy Awards and NBC's *Saturday Night Live*.

Cleveland fans hope that one day he'll be hosting a championship parade in their town!

CHAPTER THREE

THE DETROIT PISTONS

The Pistons' history is one of the most storied in all of pro basketball. It is full of championship seasons, colorful characters, and top-notch coaches—no surprise considering that the franchise is one of the oldest in the NBA. But even with all that history, there is perhaps no time like the present in Detroit.

In 2006–07, the Pistons went 53–29 during the regular season. It marked their club-record sixth consecutive year with 50 or more wins. Detroit also won the Central Division for a record-tying third time in a row that season, and for the fifth time in the last six years. The lone exception in that stretch was in 2003–04, when the Pistons finished second in the Central—then went on to win their third NBA championship!

Although Detroit's quest for its fourth league title in 2006–07 was foiled by the division-rival Cavaliers, the Pistons reached the Eastern Conference Finals for the fifth consecutive season. They also won at least one postseason series for the sixth consecutive year.

A piston is part of a car engine. Detroit didn't get its nickname because automobile manufacturing is so important to the city, though. Instead, owner Fred Zollner was a piston maker when he based the team originally in Ft. Wayne, Indiana, in 1941.

Players such as Richard Hamilton (wearing face mask) have kept the high fives going in Detroit.

All of that adds up to the lon-gest **sustained** run of excellence in the Pistons' history. And that's saying some-thing because the franchise has had a lot of good years.

The franchise began play in Fort Wayne, Indiana, in 1941. It originally was known as the Fort Wayne Zollner Pistons after founder Fred Zollner. After several

In December of 1983, the Pistons beat the Nuggets 186–184 in three overtimes in the highest-scoring game in NBA history. It came 33 years after the team (then in Ft. Wayne) beat the Minneapolis Lakers 19–18 in the lowest-scoring game ever.

years in the National Basketball League (NBL), the club joined the newly formed NBA's Central Division in 1949. The Pistons made the NBA Finals in 1955 and 1956, losing both times.

In 1957, the team relocated to Detroit. The most successful Pistons' teams of the first quarter-century in their new city came during the mid-1970s. That was when the club was led by the talented inside-outside tandem of guard Dave Bing and center Bob Lanier.

Still, the Pistons failed to win a championship until drafting the **backcourt** duo of Isiah Thomas and Joe Dumars in the 1980s. Detroit also traded wisely, picking up **big man** Bill Laimbeer and other important role players.

In 1989, all the wheeling and dealing paid off. The Pistons won 63 games—a franchise record—and the team's first-ever NBA title. Led by coach Chuck Daly, the club employed a bruising defense that earned it the nickname "Bad Boys." The Bad Boys were even badder in 1990, stomping the Portland Trail Blazers in five games in the Finals to win a second consecutive championship.

After these glory years, age caught up with some of the Pistons' best players. The franchise regained a great deal of its energy in the 1990s with the arrival of Grant Hill, a dynamic forward out of

Duke University. In 2001–02, the retooled Pistons surprised many NBA observers by winning 50 games and capturing the Central Division title. That season began their excellent current stretch.

Detroit won 50 games again and repeated as division champs the next year, then rose to the top of the NBA under Hall-of-Fame coach Larry Brown in 2003–04. Veteran forward Rasheed Wallace was a key midseason acquisition, joining players such as Ben Wallace, Richard Hamilton, Chauncey Billups, and young Tayshaun Prince. Though the roster did not feature superstars, the players blended together as a formidable team. In the Finals, the Pistons were heavy underdogs to the Lakers, but won easily in five games.

After an agonizingly close, seven-game loss to the Spurs in the Finals in 2004–05, the team hired former Timberwolves coach Flip Saunders to lead the team. Most of the core group of the championship team has remained to keep the Pistons in the driver's seat in the Motor City.

Detroit's Chuck Daly was the head coach of the United States' first "Dream Team" of NBA players at the Olympic Games in Barcelona in 1992.

Point guard *Chauncey Billups helps keep the Pistons a step ahead of the competition.*

CHAPTER FOUR

THE INDIANA PACERS

They're crazy about basketball in Indiana, and Pacers' fans routinely pack Conseco Fieldhouse.

The Pacers were the most successful franchise in the nine-year history of the American Basketball Association (ABA). The club hasn't been able to match that success since joining the NBA in 1976, but

Indiana's Darnell "Dr. Dunk" Hillman was the NBA's first slam-dunk contest champ in 1977.

it sure has come close to a championship several times.

The ABA was not a huge hit, but it was very colorful. It had a lot of interesting characters, and it played a high-scoring, freewheeling style of basketball. It also played with unique, red, white, and blue basketballs instead of the traditional orange colored ball of the NBA. Some great players, such as Hall of Famers Julius Erving and Dan Issel, got their starts in the ABA.

The Pacers were one of the original members of the ABA in 1967. They not only had a lot of success on the court, but they also built a loyal following. They drew large and enthusiastic crowds. When the league closed its doors following the 1975–76 season, Indiana was one of four ABA teams that were invited to join the NBA.

The Pacers struggled at first in the NBA. In their first 13 seasons, they posted only one winning record. Fans still came out to cheer them on, however. Billy Knight and George McGinnis were a couple of the stars of that period.

In the late 1980s, the Pacers' fortunes improved. The team added sharpshooting forward Chuck Person and a talented center from Holland, Rik Smits. Holland is a county in the country of the Netherlands. The team's most important young player, though, was guard Reggie Miller. He joined the team in 1987 from the University of California, Los Angeles (UCLA). He became one of the league's best **clutch shooters**. With this **nucleus** of players, the Pacers became championship contenders.

In 17 seasons from 1989–1990 through 2005–06, Indiana reached the playoffs all but one time. Three of those seasons—1993–94, 1994–95, and 1997–98—the team made it all the way to the Eastern Conference Finals. Though they lost all three times, Miller's heart-stopping, last-second shots excited Pacers' fans and made them feel that an NBA title was just around the corner. The team even hired Indiana basketball legend Larry Bird as coach in 1997 to make that dream a reality.

In 2000, the Pacers finally got their big chance. The team faced the Los Angeles Lakers in the NBA Finals. The Lakers, led by Shaquille O'Neal, were heavily favored. But the tough-minded Pacers would not go down easy. They fought the Lakers in a tough six-game series before losing the final game, 116–111.

It was a difficult loss to take, but the club immediately began thinking about the future. Bird gave way as coach, but became club president. Forwards Jermaine O'Neal and Ron Artest joined Miller

High school basketball is huge in Indiana. The Pacers' home, Conseco Fieldhouse, even was designed to look and feel like a high school gym.

Guard Reggie Miller was one of the best pure shooters in basketball history.

in 2000–01, and the club still made the playoffs even though it dropped to fourth place in the Central Division.

Jermaine O'Neal earned
the sixth All-Star selection
of his career in 2006–07.

After that, it was a steady climb back to the top. The Pacers finished in third place in the division in 2001–02, then in second place in 2002–03, improving their win total each season. They capped their ascent by winning a club-record 61 games

Reggie Miller's sister, Cheryl Miller, helped lead the United States to a gold medal in women's basketball at the 1984 Olympic Games.

during the regular-season in 2003–04. That gave them their first division championship since they went to the NBA Finals in 2000. O'Neal was the team's big star. He led the Pacers in both scoring (20.1 points per game) and rebounding (10.0 rebounds per game).

In the playoffs, Indiana beat the Boston Celtics and the Miami Heat. Then, the division-rival Pistons ended the Pacers' league title hopes in the conference finals.

Detroit did it again in the conference semifinals the next year. Miller retired following the 2004–05 season after a brilliant 18-year career in which he became only the 13th player in league history to amass more than 25,000 points (25,279). The Pacers eventually retired his uniform number 31.

O'Neal earned his sixth consecutive All-Star selection in 2006–07. But the club won only 35 games and missed the playoffs for the first time in 10 years. So Indiana decided it was time to retool again. Former Celtics and 76ers coach Jim O'Brien was brought in to lead the team, and Bird began tinkering with the roster.

Indiana fans hope the tuneup will have the Pacers on the road to the postseason again soon.

When they drafted center Kareem Abdul-Jabbar, the Bucks became instant championship contenders.

The history of the Milwaukee Bucks was shaped by a coin toss. Lucky for them, it came up "Milwaukee," instead of "Phoenix."

When the third-year Bucks won the 1971 NBA championship, they captured a league title quicker than any other expansion team in pro sports history.

Here's what happened. The Bucks and the Suns were expansion teams during the 1968–69 season. Not surprisingly, both clubs finished in last place in their divisions (Milwaukee in the Eastern Division and Phoenix in the Western Division), although the Bucks did win a respectable 27 games.

After the season, the NBA flipped a coin to determine which of the second-year franchises would get the first pick in the 1969 draft. Some years, the outcome might not be that big of a deal (such as in 2007, when highly touted stars Greg Oden and Kevin Durant both were coming out of college). But in 1969, the number-one choice was clear: It would be UCLA center Lew Alcindor.

Alcindor, who changed his name to Kareem Abdul-Jabbar, was one of the most dominant players in college basketball history. He had led the Bruins to three consecutive national championships. When the Bucks won the right to draft him, they were on their way to a title themselves.

Not even the most optimistic Bucks' fan could have envisioned just how quickly that championship arrived, however. With Jabbar averaging 28.8 points and 14.5 rebounds, Milwaukee soared to second place in the division in his rookie season of 1969. The team advanced to the Eastern Division

finals before losing to the eventual NBA-champion Knicks.

The next year, the Bucks traded for future Hall of Fame point guard Oscar Robertson. He was 32 years old and already had played 10 seasons in the NBA, but he was still one of the league's top all-around players. As good as he was, though, Robertson had never played for a championship team until pairing with Abdul-Jabbar. Together, the inside and outside combination propelled Milwaukee to the top of the league.

With Abdul-Jabbar averaging 31.7 points and 16.0 rebounds per game and Robertson averaging 19.4 points and 8.2 assists per game, the Bucks won 66 games and lost only 16 during the regular season. In the playoffs, neither the San Francisco Warriors, Los Angeles Lakers, nor Baltimore Bullets offered much resistance. Milwaukee won 12 games while losing only two, with a four-game sweep of the Bullets in the Finals clinching the title.

The Bucks had several more excellent seasons with Abdul-Jabbar, who was the NBA's Most Valuable Player in 1971, 1972, and 1974, in the middle. But they could not make it back to the Finals. Robertson retired following the 1973–74 season, and the big center was traded to the Lakers the next year.

Oscar Robertson is considered one of the greatest all-around players in NBA history.

In 20 seasons with the Bucks and the Los Angeles Lakers, center Kareem Abdul-Jabbar scored 38,387 career points. That's the most in NBA history.

Still, the Bucks remained a championship contender. With All-Star **swing-man** Marques Johnson leading the way, Milwaukee won the first of seven consecutive division titles in 1979–1980. The Bucks had 12 winning seasons in a row through 1990–91. Milwaukee had

In 1977, the Bucks won a game against Atlanta in which they trailed by 29 points with less than nine minutes remaining in the fourth quarter.

some playoff success in that span, too. The Bucks reached the conference finals three times, but couldn't quite make it to the NBA Finals.

Since a 48-win season in 1990–91, however, the club has had little success. One exception was in 2000–01, when guard Ray Allen and forward Glenn "Big Dog" Robinson led the team to 52 wins and a division title. Only a disappointing, seven-game loss to the 76ers for the Eastern Conference championship kept the Bucks from the NBA Finals.

Milwaukee wasn't able to build on that excellent season, though. The team fell back to a 41–41 record the next season and missed the playoffs.

The Bucks haven't won a postseason series since a seven-game victory over the Charlotte Hornets in the conference semifinals in 2001. In fact, when the club won only 28 games in 2006–07, it finished in last place in the Central Division for the third year in a row. Sharp-shooting guard Michael Redd was one of the bright spots that year. He ranked fifth in the league in scoring.

Redd's average of 26.7 points per game in 2006–07 has been bettered by only one other player in club history. That was—you guessed it—Kareem Abdul-Jabbar.

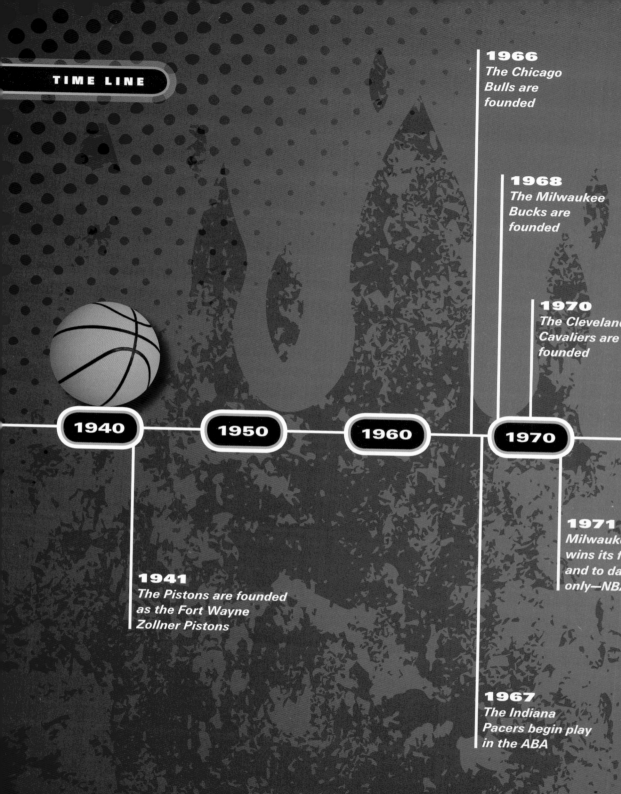

1966
The Chicago
Bulls are
founded

1968
The Milwaukee
Bucks are
founded

1970
The Cleveland
Cavaliers are
founded

1940

1950

1960

1970

1971
Milwaukee
wins its first—
and to date,
only—NBA title

1941
The Pistons are founded
as the Fort Wayne
Zollner Pistons

1967
The Indiana
Pacers begin play
in the ABA

1996
The champion Bulls set a league record by winning 72 games during the regular season

2004
Detroit beats Los Angeles in five games in the NBA Finals to win the league championship

1989
The Detroit Pistons win the first of their back-to-back NBA titles

1980

1990

2000

2010

1998
Michael Jordan wins his fifth league MVP award, and the Bulls win their sixth championship

2007
The Cavaliers reach the NBA Finals for the first time, but fall to the San Antonio Spurs

1991
Chicago wins the NBA title for the first time, and the first of three years in a row

TEAM RECORDS
(through 2006–07)

TEAM	ALL-TIME RECORD	NBA TITLES (MOST RECENT)	NUMBER OF TIMES IN PLAYOFFS	TOP COACH (WINS)
Chicago	1,703–1,626	6 (1997–98)	27	Phil Jackson (545)
Cleveland	1,349–1,653	0	15	Lenny Wilkens (316)
Detroit	2,302–2,344	3 (2003–04)	38	Chuck Daly (467)
Indiana	*1,662–1,592	*3 (1972–73)	*27	Bob Leonard (*529)
Milwaukee	1,684–1,482	1 (1970–71)	25	Don Nelson (540)

*includes ABA

MEMBERS OF THE NAISMITH MEMORIAL NATIONAL BASKETBALL HALL OF FAME

CHICAGO

PLAYER	POSITION	DATE INDUCTED
George Gervin	Guard	1996
Phil Jackson	Coach	2007
Robert Parish	Center	2003
Nate Thurmond	Center	1985

CLEVELAND

PLAYER	POSITION	DATE INDUCTED
Chuck Daly	Coach	1994
Walt "Clyde" Frazier	Guard	1987
Nate Thurmond	Center	1985
Lenny Wilkens	Guard/Coach	1989

DETROIT

PLAYER	POSITION	DATE INDUCTED
Walt Bellamy	Center	1993
Dave Bing	Guard	1990
Larry Brown	Coach	2002
Chuck Daly	Coach	1994
Dave DeBusschere	Forward	1983
Joe Dumars	Forward	2006
Harry Gallatin	Forward	1991
Bob Houbregs	Forward/Center	1987
Bailey Howell	Forward	1997
Harry "Buddy" Jeannette	Guard	1994
Bob Lanier	Center	1992
Earl Lloyd	Forward	2003
Bob McAdoo	Forward	2000
Bobby McDermott	Guard	1988
Dick McGuire	Guard	1993
Andy Phillip	Guard	1961
Isiah Thomas	Guard	2000
George Yardley	Forward	1996
Fred Zollner	Owner	1999

CENTRAL DIVISION CAREER LEADERS
(through 2006–07)

TEAM	CATEGORY	NAME (YEARS WITH TEAM)	TOTAL
Chicago	Points	Michael Jordan (1984–1993, 1994–1998)	29,277
	Rebounds	Michael Jordan (1984–1993, 1994–1998)	5,836
Cleveland	Points	Brad Daugherty (1986–1996)	10,389
	Rebounds	Brad Daugherty (1986–1996)	5,227
Detroit	Points	Isiah Thomas (1981–1994)	18,822
	Rebounds	Bill Laimbeer (1981–1994)	9,430
Indiana	Points	Reggie Miller (1987–2005)	25,279
	Rebounds	Mel Daniels (1968–1974)	7,643
Milwaukee	Points	Kareem Abdul-Jabbar (1969–1975)	14,211
	Rebounds	Kareem Abdul-Jabbar (1969–1975)	7,161

INDIANA

PLAYER	POSITION	DATE INDUCTED
Larry Brown	Coach	2002
Alex English	Forward	1997
Jack Ramsay	Coach	1992

MILWAUKEE

PLAYER	POSITION	DATE INDUCTED
Kareem Abdul-Jabbar	Center	1995
Nate "Tiny" Archibald	Guard	1991
Dave Cowens	Center	1991
Alex English	Forward	1997
Bob Lanier	Center	1992
Moses Malone	Center	2001
Oscar Robertson	Guard	1980

backcourt—in this instance, a term for the guards in a team's lineup; it also refers to the area on a basketball court from the centerline to the baseline that a team defends

big man—another term for center

clutch shooters—players who are skilled at making especially timely or difficult shots

draft—the annual selection of college players by a professional sports league

expansion team—a new franchise that starts from scratch

franchise—more than just the team, it is the entire organization that is a member of a professional sports league

heyday—time of greatest success

jumper—a shot in which a player jumps into the air and releases the ball from above his head; also called a jump shot

magnitude—in astronomy, the brightness of a star or other object

nucleus—the core group of players around which a team is built

playoffs—a four-level postseason elimination tournament involving eight teams for each conference; levels include the first round, a conference semifinal round, a conference championship round, and the NBA Finals (all series are best-of-seven games)

point guard—the player who brings the ball upcourt for the offensive team

postseason—another name for the playoffs; a team must make it through three rounds to reach the NBA Finals

rebuilding—the process of building a team back up again after a period of poor play

role players—players who specialize in one or two aspects of the game, such as defense or rebounding

sustained—kept up or prolonged over a period of time

swingman—a player capable of playing either guard or forward

FOR MORE INFORMATION ABOUT THE CENTRAL DIVISION AND THE NBA

Books

Hareas, John. *Basketball.* New York: DK Publishers, 2005.

Leboutillier, Nate. *The Story of the Chicago Bulls.* Mankato, Minnesota: Creative Education, 2006.

Leboutillier, Nate. *The Story of the Cleveland Cavaliers.* Mankato, Minnesota: Creative Education, 2006.

Leboutillier, Nate. *The Story of the Milwaukee Bucks.* Mankato, Minnesota: Creative Education, 2006.

Miller, Raymond H. *Michael Jordan.* San Diego: Kidhaven Press, 2003.

Stewart, Mark. *The Indiana Pacers.* Chicago: Norwood House Press, 2007.

Stewart, Mark. *LeBron James.* Chicago: Raintree, 2005.

Stewart, Mark. *The NBA Finals.* New York: Franklin Watts, 2003.

Stewart, Mark, and Zeysing, Matt. *The Detroit Pistons.* Chicago: Norwood House Press, 2006.

On the Web

Visit our Web page for lots of links about the Central Division teams: *http://www.childsworld.com/links*

NOTE TO PARENTS, TEACHERS, AND LIBRARIANS: We routinely verify our Web links to make sure they are safe, active sites—so encourage your readers to check them out!

ABOUT THE AUTHORS

James S. Kelley is the pseudonym for a group of veteran sportswriters who collaborated on this series. Among them, they have worked for *Sports Illustrated*, the National Football League, and NBC Sports. They have written more than a dozen other books for young readers on a wide variety of sports.